UNSTOPPABLE

Strategies to Launch and Grow your Holistic Practice

Michelle McGlade

Published by Best Seller Publishing, Pasadena, CA

Best Seller Publishing® is a registered trademark

Printed in the United States of America.

ISBN _________

LCCN: ________

For more information, please write:

Best Seller Publishing

1346 Walnut Street, #205

Pasadena, CA 91106

or call 1(626) 765 9750

Toll Free: 1(844) 850-3500

Visit us online at: www.BestSellerPublishing.org

Table of Contents

Acknowledgements

Throughout my life, I have enjoyed placing myself in situations where I am surrounded by talented and supportive individuals. This endeavor has been no different.

Thank you, Sunniva Neyland and the entire team who have been my writing and publishing cohorts.

A special note of gratitude to those who provided feedback helping me to polish and shine: Maureen Feeney, Carolyn Hatch, Naomi Marietta, and Tom Niemiec. And especially Wendy Robson, who honored me with her magical edits to the very last drop.

Finally, thank you to the man who makes my dreams come true, Neal Niemiec.

Introduction

Every holistic practitioner I meet is extremely passionate about helping others. We all have our unique talents as healers, and many of us have a powerful story and journey of finding our career in holistic healthcare.

As the wellness industry continues to grow, and the demand for our professions increases, we need to be better positioned and prepared to lead within our industry, yet so many of us are struggling just to make it.

It is my desire to share my experiences and knowledge with you to help close this gap. This book was written to build your knowledge and skill in the foundational concepts of business. Once we align strong business skills and execution with our passion for helping and healing others, I believe we will be truly unstoppable. If you are a passionate healer and new practitioner who is feeling overwhelmed and alone, or a practitioner who is not making the money you desire and deserve and who does not know where to start, then this book is going to give you the tools to create a profitable, growing and admired business.

In the following pages, I will bring you beyond your passion by providing you the key business elements you need to raise your skill sets and accelerate the growth of your holistic practice.

While no book can be a fully definitive resource on any topic, if you stay with me from cover to cover, you will learn more about how to do the following:

- Identify and leverage your strengths to grow your practice;
- Improve your leadership skills to position you as the expert in your community;
- Assemble a solid team to provide the support structure you need for lasting success;
- Set goals and create a plan to provide accountability and focused execution;
- Orchestrate a client experience that will earn loyalty so that clients stay with you and provide referrals;
- Establish processes and tracking methods to mitigate risk;
- Simplify your marketing efforts, so you are focused and attracting your ideal clients;
- Lead your clients through a buying decision that does not feel sales-y and increases client compliance with your treatment plan;

- And evaluate and document your progress, so you stay on track.

Let's turn your passion into productivity and profitability! Your passion provides the spark and momentum for your practice. But it is the right tools, the right focus, and the right business skills that will accelerate the growth of your holistic practice and drive measurable results. Are you ready to be unstoppable? Let's begin.

Section 1

People

CHAPTER 1

TAKE A SELFIE

"Leading with your strengths and placing yourself in opportunities where you can show off and shine place you ahead of the competition."

One of my favorite things about owning a business is that it's all about the people. When I first started out, I may have said something more like "It's all about the clients." Getting and keeping clients is extremely important, but now I know that it's about so much more than that.

It's about the practitioners that you work alongside. It's about the business colleagues you associate with. It's about the community you work and live in, your employees, and the industry that you participate in. Most importantly, it's all about you. Everything from starting up to owning and growing a successful practice is based on the foundation of you.

As a business owner, you need to take an intimate look at your strengths and weaknesses. It is also important to consider how you structure your business and create structure within your business to ensure that it coincides with your desired lifestyle. Finally, you need to consider how you define success for yourself and how you celebrate it.

UNDERSTANDING YOUR STRENGTHS AND WEAKNESSES

> **ACTION INTO PRACTICE**
>
> *Make a list of your strengths and ensure to seek feedback from at least five different sources.*

One of my favorite sayings is: "If you want to get to know yourself, then start a business." As a business owner, you will continually become more self-aware. You will continually learn and grow both personally and professionally. This is inevitable; however, the more you know yourself and work to leverage your strengths and surround yourself with individuals who fill your gaps, the stronger foundation you will create for your business.

If you have not done so already, it is imperative you complete an honest assessment of your strengths and weaknesses. Even if you think you have a good grasp of what your strengths and weaknesses might be, it is valuable to check back in. Seek also out counsel from others to ensure your perceptions are correct.

When I was in startup mode as a business owner, the first thing I did was put together an honest inventory of my strengths and weaknesses. I was already familiar with StrengthsFinder *(www.strengthsfinder.com) by Tom Rath. I had used it in my corporate career, and I found the endeavor to be worthwhile and fairly accurate, so I started my journey with an updated assessment.*

Like most of you, I already had a fairly good idea of some of my strengths and weaknesses based on my past experiences, so I added this information to my list. Then I sought feedback from trusted sources such as my husband, a few close friends, and my colleagues. I even gathered feedback from some of my clients.

The list of my strengths and weaknesses compiled through this process has served me extremely well over the years, and I continue to refine it. I successfully built my holistic practice based on it, and I have continued to leverage my strengths for success. Below I will provide some examples.

Leveraging Your Strengths

After being in business for two years, with my practice in full swing, I became extremely selective with my time. One of the marketing activities that continued to be effective was teaching educational classes in the community for a fee. These classes resulted in exposure and an opportunity for my practice. A local cable channel approached me to record my class and air it for their audience. However, I realized the individuals paying for the class might not be as forthcoming during the class if they knew it was being recorded. For that reason, I respectfully declined.

But when the producer asked if I would be willing to come into the studio and record the class sans students, I accepted the offer. By the end of the recording, the producer and I had formed a great connection, and she asked if she could bring her team to my clinic and interview me about the clinic and the services that were offered.

From the outside, it might look a bit like luck, but everything about this was intentional. The reason I was teaching classes was because I love public speaking, and I'm aware I excel at it. It was a way to build my brand, drive referrals, and make money by using one of my strengths.

As a result, I was provided the opportunity to create a video recording of the class. Without spending any money, my clinic gained exposure, and I received a professionally made video I could now use to educate my clients and promote my practice.

ACTION INTO PRACTICE

Identify three marketing activities you can do that leverage your strengths.

Since I spoke well and had established a relationship with the producer, I secured another opportunity to generate exposure for the clinic. It came via an interview, which yielded another professionally produced video that I could now leverage for marketing purposes.

I am not suggesting this path for everyone. I use this story to show how leading with your strengths and placing yourself in opportunities where you can show off and shine while doing what you love place you ahead of the competition.

Filling in the Gaps

> **Action into Practice**
>
> *Identify three things you do not excel at in your business that you can outsource, allowing you to spend more time doing what you love.*

When I had been in business for one year, I decided to seek business mentorship. Based on my business plans and goals for growth, my mentors advised it would be critical to document the processes and procedures of the clinic. Otherwise, the speed of my growth would be limited. Their advice was to slow down in the short-term, so I would be in a better position to move more quickly in the long-term.

I understood the importance of documenting the processes and procedures, but I had avoided completing this project to date. It was de-motivating to me to spend time in this way, so I had simply chosen not to do it.

Three months later, I hired my first employee. This prompted a first attempt at writing down some of the processes and procedures of the day-to-day flow at the clinic.

However, my effort was not longstanding. Fortunately, when I finally made the decision to add administrative support at the clinic, I was able to hire someone to not only help take care of our clients and the day-to-day office management but also assist with the development of our operational manual.

It was clear to me who I needed to hire. I knew my strengths, and I knew my weaknesses. I hired for the gap. I hired a process-oriented person who loved and excelled at putting together documentation, processes, and procedures.

CREATING A BUSINESS STRUCTURE THAT FITS YOU

Knowing your strengths and weaknesses is part of the foundation of building a successful practice, but it also means understanding how you need to structure your business to meet your desired lifestyle. Understanding what you want and why you want it, and then developing a business structure to support you is a step that is often missed. Getting clear on what you want and why provides clarity for your business structure. It also allows for clear decision-making, provides motivation, and ensures you are considering how to balance work, family, friends, and financial and spiritual health – your overall wellbeing.

The role of business owner will continually challenge the balance of your life. For that reason, it's extremely important to take a look at how all of the areas of your life interact and think about how you would like them to interact. Then you need to adjust your business structure to support this.

When I started my clinic, I sought to create a multi-disciplinary model. I wanted it to be a place where practitioners would come together and collaborate on behalf of the clients. I was highly aware that to accomplish this vision, I would only be able to work as a practitioner about 10 to 15 hours a week. The rest of my time would be spent working as clinic owner managing and leading the business. I also knew that I might have to work seven days a week, especially early on.

ACTION INTO PRACTICE

Write down what you desire from your holistic practice and then clearly identify why you desire it.

It meant that if I were not bringing in enough income to pay my bills or make payroll, I would potentially have to use my personal savings to cover those costs. It also meant that I might not be able to take a vacation, especially in the beginning. Or if I did take time off, I would still be the individual on call if any issue arose at the clinic. For example, once water flooded into the clinic, and as the clinic owner, it was my responsibility to deal with that.

The awareness of all of the different roles I would have to fill was extremely important. I knew it would affect me individually and could challenge my health. It would also place pressure on my time. This would affect my family, and it could affect my relationships with friends. The important part was to keep my eyes wide open, realize it was the kind of business I wanted, and be aware of what it would require of me.

Creating a business structure that not only helps you achieve what you want but also matches your lifestyle is imperative. I have spoken with many practitioners who started their own business because they thought it was what they wanted; later discovering that being a business owner did not align with their desired lifestyle.

Defining Success

Understanding yourself and creating structure sets you up for success. Success is a foundational component of creating a business that you love, and it drives a practice.

Many practitioners are paralyzed by the fear of not achieving. They look at their colleagues and others in the industry and get trapped in the game of comparing. What you can do instead is define and redefine what success looks like for yourself. Let me provide an example.

Six months after I opened my clinic, I had the opportunity to purchase another business, and I went ahead and did so. The business model for the second clinic differed from my first business, so I created a separate brand for it and hired two talented practitioners to run it. It turned out to be very successful. A well-known magazine in the area wrote about it, and it received local recognition. However, after nine months, I closed it. This decision was made because managing multiple locations placed too much demand on my time.

From an outside perspective, that might seem like a failure. But I chose to define it as a success for several reasons. First, I took a risk. As an entrepreneur, it is extremely important to take risks.

Second, I learned that having multiple brick-and-mortar locations did not fit my desired lifestyle. This was extremely valuable information because my original business plan was to have multiple locations for my clinic. Having had two locations led me to understand that it would not be a good fit for me in the long-term.

Third, it provided me the experience of hiring and firing employees. I was able to begin creating processes and procedures for the clinic (which we now know that I don't love).

> **ACTION INTO PRACTICE**
>
> *What goal are you working toward in your holistic practice right now? Make a commitment to yourself on how you will celebrate once you achieve it!*

Finally, through the experience came innovation. I ended up transitioning the clients I had at my second location to my original location, which was only 4 miles away. I did that by creating an express acupuncture service offering for them.

I received the great opportunity to learn, early on, that you need to define success for yourself. Instead of saying something is a success or failure; I now say it's all about choice. You make the best choice you can at any given time. Each choice is based on what you have experienced and learned; as well as what is right for your lifestyle along with considering your strengths and weaknesses.

I also learned that celebrating milestones is extremely important. Business owners are often looking forward to the larger goals they desire to meet, and as they accomplish them, they are typically already on to the next goal. I am guilty of doing this and have seen the same behaviors in the business owners I advise. They forget to look at all that has been accomplished and, as a result, end up feeling like they are constantly failing. Stopping to celebrate milestones large and small is extremely important because business ownership is a constant growth process.

A strong foundation is essential to a successful business, no matter what industry you are in, and it holds true for holistic practitioners as well. To build a strong foundation for your business and be successful, you need to "take a selfie." Play to your strengths and fill in the gaps where you have weaknesses, create a business structure that fits your desired lifestyle, and define what success looks like for you And celebrate often!

CHAPTER 2

BECOME A SUPERHERO

"Investing in leadership activities is the difference between a business owner and a successful business owner."

You have now had the chance to take a look in the mirror to evaluate and assess yourself. You need to take one more peek because the focus still has to be on you.

This time, however, you need to think about who you want to become as a business owner and how you choose to do it. It's all about being a leader. Successful business owners not only acknowledge they have a role as leaders; they choose and embrace leadership.

As a practitioner, you play a leadership role in the care of your clients. You advocate on behalf of the client, and you are a leader in their plan of care. As an expert in your field, you may even play a role of leadership in your industry.

As a business owner, you have a greater role to play. In addition to playing a leadership role for your clients, or within the industry, you can also be a leader in the community where you live and work, for your business, the colleagues you work alongside, and your employees. Successful business ownership requires leadership.

LEADERSHIP AND MANAGEMENT

There is a clear difference between leadership and management. A manager has individuals who work with them administering the day-to-day operations of a business. A leader has people who follow them, and those who follow have a great understanding and strong belief in the vision of their leader.

A manager will monitor operations. They look at whether sales are up or down, what is going right and what is going wrong, and whether everyone is doing their job. A leader, on the other hand, uncovers opportunity, inspires with a vision, and builds relationships.

> **ACTION INTO PRACTICE**
>
> *What percentage of your day do you spend on leadership activities versus management activities in your practice?*

A manager will have individuals on their team who come to them for advice. It is often referred to as a circle of power. A leader will also have individuals who seek their advice. These individuals may be on the leader's team or from positions and areas outside the team. This is often referred to as a circle of influence.

Managers plan and budget. They make staffing decisions, and they measure and solve problems. A leader looks for opportunities. They will create a vision and gain team buy-in, empower people, and produce change through actions.

Both the manager and the leader are keen on flawless execution. Both of them understand the importance of people, and both of them are responsible for directing resources.

The truth is that as a business owner, you need to both lead and manage your business. Those of you who can effectively create a balance between leadership activities and management activities in the day-to-day operations of your businesses will create the greatest competitive advantage.

I realized very early on that I would not only need to be a fabulous practitioner, but I would also need to manage the day-to-day operations of my business effectively, and I would have to be a relentless leader. I had to become a superhero.

Think about it: Wonder Woman, Batman, and Superman are extraordinary. They go beyond the norm. They are transformative. They create change in the communities where they work and live. They have allies. They create mutually beneficial relationships and bring people together for a common cause. Of course, we know they have superhuman powers, and don't forget; they all have a day job.

Two Approaches

Let me share the stories of two wellness business owners. They are very similar stories at the start, but if you pay attention, you will see how they become very different towards the end.

The name of the first business owner is Jenny. She has been practicing for three years.

When Jenny graduated, she knew she wanted to start her own business, so she contracted space. She developed a nice-looking logo, put it on her business card, and put up a website.

Jenny normally works from 9 am to 5 pm, 40 hours a week. In her typical day, she will arrive at her clinic around 9 am. She will spend an hour or so setting up for the day, checking email, and returning phone calls. She will see two to four clients before lunch. Then she will take a break. After lunch, she will see one to three clients.

Before she heads home for the day at 5 pm, she works on some administrative tasks and manages the day-to-day operations. She might complete the insurance billing and order supplies for the clinic. Perhaps she will do a couple marketing activities like posting on Facebook or writing a blog for her website. She may even have time to read an article or two in an industry magazine.

Although Jenny has been in business for three years, she does not have a steady flow of clients yet, so it wouldn't be unusual for her to have a couple of free hours in her day. During these free hours, she chooses to stay in the office and focus on educational activities that will improve her skills as a practitioner.

Jenny, in her third year in business, is now able to make her rent and pay her bills on time. She also pays herself an annual salary of about $30,000.

Now let me share Sarah's story with you. Sarah and Jenny started their businesses at the same time. Just like Jenny, Sarah wanted to start her own business, so she contracted space, developed a nice-looking logo and business card, and put up a website. Sarah also works about 40 hours a week in her clinic.

However, Sarah sees between 8 and 10 clients a day and is booked out three weeks in advance. She has very limited time to work on the administrative duties in her clinic, but she manages to get it all done in about 40 hours a week.

Sarah works an additional 10 to 20 hours a week. During these extra work hours, she attends one to three networking events each week. She meets with her business mentors on a regular basis to review her progress, revise her business plan, talk about her strategy, and plan for growth. She often has one to two meetings each week or at least a phone call with other practitioners who regularly reach out to her for advice and guidance on how to ensure success.

In addition, Sarah is meeting with other practitioners in her area on a regular basis because they plan a monthly marketing open house for their community. Lastly, Sarah provides an educational seminar at her local community center once a week.

Like Jenny, Sarah can make rent and pay her bills on time. However, Sarah can provide herself a salary of $100,000 a year.

The difference between Jenny and Sarah is that Sarah understands that not only do you have to be a great practitioner and manage the day-to-day activities of your business, but you also need to invest time in leadership activities. Sarah is working her day job, but she has found a way to balance the role of the practitioner with the role of business owner.

Sarah also understands that she needs to leverage her "superhuman powers," which are her strengths. To do this, she does speaking engagements in her community. She has formed allies; she has created mutually beneficial relationships with other practitioners in her area to help provide value to their community and grow their businesses. Just as superheroes join together to overcome their challenges, Sarah has made this behavior of finding others and working with them a best practice.

Sarah strives to be transformative. She is working on creating a plan for growth in her business and is accelerating change by finding business mentorship. She challenges herself to be extraordinary by going beyond the norms of what other practitioners are doing. She is recognized by her peers who regularly reach out to her for guidance. Sarah is a superhero.

ACTION INTO PRACTICE

Identify three leadership activities you are doing or could be doing that leverage your strengths.

Practitioners often approach me to learn how I have achieved success, and I share with them the stories of Jenny and Sarah. Their stories illustrate the business owners I have talked with and the types of behaviors they exhibit as leaders who have contributed to their long-term success.

Learning from Struggle

The best learning doesn't come just from stories of success. It also comes from stories of struggle. You may recall that I talked about purchasing another clinic. My story with this clinic started out very similarly to both Jenny and Sarah.

I had to renegotiate the lease for the contracted space. I developed a brand-new logo and a business card, and I put up a website just like they did. I was smart enough to know that I needed help since it was a second business for me, so I hired individuals to work as practitioners and manage the day-to-day activities of the clinic. My plan was to work on the leadership activities. I wanted to leverage my strengths in the community and be as much of a superhero as I could. What happened, however, is a different story.

> **Action into Practice**
>
> *What percent of your time is spent working in your practice versus working on your business?*

Over several months, I began getting things up and running at the second clinic. As I redirected my focus and spent more time on this location to ensure its success, my first location started to fail. It occurred to me that I better let the individuals I had hired take the lead at the second clinic and switch my focus back to my original business location. But guess what? Then the second location started to fail. I knew the recipe for success, but I had not created an effective balance or shared this recipe.

So I did what a leader needs to do, and I made a decision: I closed the second clinic location. I wrote it off as a learning experience and moved on. I didn't look back on the loss or the time spent and lament "if only."

The key is not just focusing on being a great practitioner and managing day-to-day operations. You also need to invest in leadership activities, which is what makes the difference between a business owner and a *successful* business owner.

When I talk with holistic practitioners about how they are going to accomplish everything their business demands, we also talk about creating a balance between working *in* their business and working *on* their business. Truly successful business ownership comes from balance.

CHAPTER 3

DESIGN YOUR TEAM

"As a business owner, your network is your team. Carefully designing your team is a critical element of success,"

At this stage, I have made a strong case for why creating a successful holistic practice begins and ends with you. But if you recall, I started by saying I believe that it's all about the people. Now we are finally ready to talk about the individuals you choose to place around you.

Starting, owning, and growing a successful practice takes a small army, and there is no way you can do it with an army of one. There are four critical roles you will want to fill when you design your team. These are the inner circle, your trusted advisers, your circle of influence, and your everyday "peeps."

The Inner Circle

Let's first talk about the individuals who will be part of your inner circle. These are your champions. They believe in you. Even if they don't fully understand all the aspects of your business, they still have your back. They are your greatest cheerleaders and will provide the pep talk you need when you feel down.

Many of the business owners I advise say they feel isolated. Having these team members will provide you with support. You can talk to them about your challenges and your greatest fears, and they can give you advice and reassurances that you are not alone.

> **ACTION INTO PRACTICE**
>
> *Identify three individuals who are part of your inner circle.*

A common error many practitioners make is that they assume certain people are going to fill these roles. For example, your partner or spouse is not automatically on the team. Your sister, your best friend, even your spiritual adviser do not get to join your team unless you decide you want them. Find three or four individuals who can be part of your inner circle to provide you the support you will need throughout the ups and downs of business ownership.

So who is in my inner circle? My husband is my number one fan and coach, and he has a fabulously creative mind. Another person in my inner circle is an acupuncture colleague who I met in school. We started our businesses around the same time. I also have a college friend who understands me very well. Finally, in my inner circle is another business owner outside my industry. I met this person in my early days as a business owner. We hit it off, and we have been challenging and supporting one another along the way.

I chose these individuals first and foremost because I love and admire them. They may not know all the ins and outs of my business, but they know me. They are the people I go to with my highs and lows, my challenges, and my fears. They offer me advice and guidance. Their advice isn't just focused on where I am today, but it is based on their understanding of me and where I want to go. They have an unwavering belief in me even when I have lost belief in myself.

Trusted Advisers

Remember how we talked about knowing your strengths and weaknesses? Your trusted advisers are typically the experts who can help to fill your gaps. These individuals also coach or counsel you in your business decisions. Having these trusted advisers will bring you peace of mind and reassurance.

Since you probably will pay a fee for expert services, I advise you to shop around and interview people for these spots on your team. You want to ensure the expertise they bring meets your needs and that they have a good understanding of your business and industry.

Many business owners make the mistake of waiting to hire these experts until the moment they need them. Instead, you want to identify potential trusted advisers early on. That way, you can develop a relationship with them. When the need arises, you know exactly who to call, and they will not have to spend time getting up the learning curve on what your business does.

I identified different trusted advisers by using my network and asking for referrals. Early on in my business, before I had clients, I went out and met people in different settings such as the local Chamber of Commerce and the Rotary. This is where I met some of the individuals that became trusted advisers.

I advise you to have an accountant, an attorney, a relationship with a financial institution or at least a commercial loan officer, and a business mentor. You may also have trusted advisers that you outsource to, for example, a bookkeeper or administrative support.

ACTION INTO PRACTICE

Identify who you will contact when you need:

- *Tax advice*
- *Legal advice*
- *Financial support*
- *Business advice*

My trusted advisers have helped me in a variety of ways. My attorney encouraged me to start my clinic before I was planning to, seeing something in me I had not yet seen in myself. He also helped me negotiate lease terms and turn down an employment opportunity that wasn't in my best interest. My accountant helped me develop a compensation structure for independent contractors. My bank provided me a loan for a growth opportunity even when I didn't have positive net revenues. My business mentors have challenged me on the tough issues and supported my decisions in those matters. They have also connected me with other trusted advisers when I did not know where to turn.

There are endless ways these individuals can assist.

Circle of Influence

The next critical group of individuals to have on your team is your circle of influence. This is a much larger and more fluid group of individuals. These are people who you network with in the community where you work or live or both.

Within this network, you can identify key people who you develop mutual respect and trust with over time. These are the individuals who you want to add to your team. Look for opportunities to collaborate with them to find win-win scenarios to grow both of your businesses. They could be individuals within your industry, but they don't have to be. More importantly, they are business owners, working professionals, or even community leaders.

When you are identifying people for this team, think about quality over quantity, especially if you are out networking, creating momentum for your business, and achieving fabulous results. Many people will gravitate towards you, and they will want to work with you. You want to identify those who are not only looking to share the results but will also share the effort to help build results for you both. It's also important to consider their reputation because it will reflect on yours and vice-versa. I always choose people I admire.

Over time, I have met people who carry themselves in a way I respect and treat me the way I want to treat my clients. When I identify these people, I ask them to a one-on-one lunch or breakfast meeting to get to know them better and see if there is an opportunity for us to leverage both of our skill sets for a mutually beneficial outcome. Below are several examples.

Through my network I, came to know a female business owner in the cosmetic industry. Every year, she hosts a holiday open house for her clients. Since we have a lot of respect for and trust in each other, one year, we decided that she would host her holiday open house at my clinic. She invited her clients, and I invited mine. This allowed us to co-mingle our clients and expose both of our brands in a more effective way by allowing existing clients to serve as brand ambassadors for our respective businesses.

As an acupuncture practitioner, I made an effort to get to know other holistic practitioners in my area. Early on, I identified two chiropractors and one massage therapist. Month after month, year after year, we provided referrals for one another. As our relationship developed, our trust in and support for each other grew. Then, if I was hosting an event at the clinic or needed to do larger announcements locally, they were often willing to send my communications out to their lists as well. And, when appropriate, I did the same for them.

ACTION INTO PRACTICE

Identify three individuals you will approach to establish a mutually beneficial partnership.

When I opened my clinic, I hosted a grand opening. At this grand opening, I collected donations on behalf of a non-profit organization meaningful to me. It was another way to create a mutually beneficial partnership while providing additional exposure for my business.

Once or twice a year, I brought together everyone in my circle of influence for a networking event at my clinic; giving them an opportunity to meet other people. I'm extremely passionate about partnering and creating connections, and this attribute is a huge key to my success.

Your circle of influence is developed over time. You can find networking opportunities by using Meetup.com, visiting a Rotary, or getting involved with your local Chamber of Commerce. You can also use BNI, Business Networking International (www.bni.com). This is a fairly well-known, fee-based networking opportunity where the primary focus of the members is to support and network with one another's businesses. I have never been an official member of a BNI chapter, but I have attended many meetings. The important thing is finding the group that fits you best.

Every opportunity is a networking opportunity. If you find that professional networking groups are not a fit for you, consider other options. You could, for example, start or join a book club, volunteer, get involved in your local government, or take a seat on a board of directors. Any place where you can interact with leaders in your community is a place to develop relationships that can be mutually beneficial.

Action into Practice

Who are your everyday "peeps" who are influencing your clients?

Everyday Peeps

Your everyday "peeps" are the people you can potentially hire and fire. They could be employees, but they don't necessarily have to be. It could be anybody who you work alongside in your day-to-day business. It could, for example, be other practitioners, a receptionist, or an office manager. If you have independent contractors, employees, or people subleasing from you, then you are in a position to hire and fire.

When you hire these people, don't just look at their skill sets. You also need to assess whether they will be a fit for your business based on culture and values. This group of people will require ongoing coaching about your brand so they can mimic and match what you offer.

Some of you might say, "Well, I'm a solo practitioner. I don't hire and fire people, so this does not apply to me." That is not necessarily true. If you are a solo business owner, and you work all alone in a rented space, then perhaps it does not apply. But even as a solo business owner you need to interact with other people and businesses. I advise many business owners that are subleasing space inside the offices of another business. It's important to understand how that business's employees conduct themselves because they are going to interact with your clients. The health of your business can be affected positively or negatively by these interactions.

Early on, I was looking to expand my business into another market, so I considered subleasing space in a chiropractic office. Prior to finalizing the contract, I found out that someone who had worked for that chiropractor experienced poor treatment as an employee. After further consideration and research, I turned down the opportunity because I wasn't completely confident in the chiropractor's interactions with my clients, and I didn't want to take the chance of this person's actions reflecting poorly on my brand.

As a holistic health practitioner and small business owner, your network is your team. You need to be thoughtful about who you choose for your inner circle, trusted advisers, circle of influence, and everyday "peeps." Carefully designing your team is a critical element of success, and it's all about the people. It's not just who you know, but it's also how well you know them, along with how well you know yourself.

SECTION 2

PROCESSES

Chapter 4

Date Night with Your Business Plan

"It's the process of writing and planning that has the most value, not the actual business plan itself."

Early success in business ownership begins with the people. Lasting success is determined by the process. The process is simply a series of actions that will produce positive, repeatable reactions.

As practitioners, you apply this concept on a daily basis with your clients. No matter what your modality, you often develop a treatment plan – a course of action – that will produce positive outcomes for most clients.

As a business owner, you need to think about all aspects of your business in terms of processes. Whether they concern business planning, creating a client experience or even the day-to-day operations of your business, the processes are non-negotiable, so it's time to embrace and celebrate them.

Your first exposure to processes for your practice should have been business planning. Yes, I'm talking about the dreaded business plan that most of you probably are too intimidated to write. Or if you did write a business plan, it might be because you had to in school. In that case, it most likely doesn't even apply to your practice at this time. Or perhaps you are one of the very few who did start writing a business plan but likely never finished it. Either way, if you have a written business plan, when was the last time you looked at it? It's time to put aside your feelings of intimidation and become a believer in the power and the process of business planning.

WHY BUSINESS PLANNING?

Numbers don't lie. Statistics show that the success rate of your business will increase if you have a written business plan. Anywhere from 40 to 75 percent of all businesses fail within the first year, and over half fail within the first three years. Many business owners I advise fear their business will never make money. An important part of overcoming that fear is the preparation of a business plan.

Many practitioners also express a lack of confidence in their knowledge of business, and they struggle with what to do and how to do it. By preparing a business plan, you have the opportunity to find out if your business idea is viable and, most importantly, if you can make money with it.

Business planning alleviates some of the burdens of feeling overwhelmed. Once you know that your business idea is viable, business planning allows you to organize the steps you need to take to achieve the financial results you desire. Additionally, business plans can help clarify and simplify critical decisions. If you are presented with an opportunity, you can evaluate it against your plan to see if it helps or if it's a distraction or even a risk to your business. In fact saying, "No" to good things is sometimes necessary so that you can do a few things great and accomplish the goals for your business.

Similar to your treatment plan, if a client follows only 25 percent of the plan you have outlined, the results will not be as certain as if the client were to follow 100 percent of the steps outlined in your treatment plan.

Writing a business plan is also a process of setting goals and determining the steps necessary to reach those goals. It will help define what you want to achieve and what it takes to get there. It also provides you an opportunity to identify any gaps. Knowing where you are vulnerable or where you have a lack of knowledge will help you with your decisions moving forward. For example, it can help you identify what type of trusted advisers you might want to hire.

I'm not suggesting that you put together a five-year, 80-page glossy booklet with graphs and photos. If you are seeking money from a bank or an investor, you will need to consider a formal plan. But for the majority of holistic practitioners, a well thought-out plan with bullet points and a few handwritten worksheets will suffice. It's the process of writing and planning that has the most value, not the actual business plan itself.

GETTING STARTED

Before writing a complete business plan, there are four exercises that I recommend you complete.

Your ideal practice. The first one is a writing exercise. Grab a pen and paper and use words to paint a picture of your ideal business. Talk about where it's located and who else might be there working alongside you. Describe how it looks and feels when you walk through the door. Next, discuss why you want to start a business. What does owning a business mean to you? Finally, share why you are specifically equipped to make this business a success.

Financial feasibility. Once you have completed the writing activity, the next step is to assess your business idea using a very basic financial equation. Write down on a piece of paper the number of hours you will work each month. Multiply that number by the hourly rate you plan to charge. Take that resulting number and subtract your monthly expenses. Now, what is left over? Is there any money or not? That is the amount you may be able to pay yourself. Remember, this includes all time spent working in and on your business – client care, as well as time spent

> **ACTION INTO PRACTICE**
>
> *Financial feasibility equation:*
> *Number of hours per month x*
> *rate per hour – monthly expenses = ?*

on marketing, administrative activities, accounting, etc. This number tells you if you have a viable business opportunity.

Interviews. The third exercise is to complete interviews. Find three or four business owners in your industry to interview. Reach 10 to 15 miles or more outside your local market, so they are not in direct competition, but be certain to interview people within your industry.

> **ACTION INTO PRACTICE**
>
> *Identify three business owners within your industry but outside your market who you will request to interview.*

Over the years, I have had the opportunity to be interviewed by a lot of promising practitioners, and I'm always very welcoming when they ask if they can meet with me. I'm excited to talk about my business to anyone who will listen. Unfortunately, the practitioners often fail to take advantage of the ways I can help during these meetings. Why? This is an opportunity to gather as much information as possible, yet many practitioners do not ask the right questions.

When you have the opportunity to meet with other business owners in your industry, you want to gather valuable information you can use in your business planning process. It's important to ask things like:

- What is their competitive advantage?
- How do they view their strengths and weakness compared to their competitors?
- How do they price their services?

- Why are their services priced the way they are?
- How do they get and keep clients on a regular basis?
- What were their startup costs?
- What monthly costs do they incur to run their business?

All of this information is extremely valuable to you. You do not want to miss out on the opportunity to gather the information you need when you meet with these business owners.

Present to experts. The final exercise before beginning the process of writing your business plan is to bring the information you have gathered to your experts. This is a perfect time to seek advice from your business mentors, the valuable members of your trusted advisers team. When you review the information you have gathered together with your experts, they can provide feedback and direction before you get too far in your planning. This early course correction can save you valuable time and energy. One of my favorite resources is a national organization called SCORE (www.score.org). They offer free support, tools, and mentorship for small businesses.

Now you have imagined your dream practice, done a quick financial evaluation, interviewed business owners, and discussed all of this information with your trusted advisers. Fabulous! Your business plan is closer to being done than you realize.

Key Elements of a Business Plan

Now let's discuss some of the key elements you will need to get down on paper to make a great business plan and set you up for lasting success as a holistic practitioner.

Business overview. If you completed the exercises that I suggested and did an evaluation of your strengths and weaknesses, you are going to be well positioned to put together a complete business overview. First and foremost, you want to talk about what kind of business you are going to start. You will include why you want to start this business and how you are positioning the business to make it a success. You may also include the structure of your business and outline achievable and measurable goals for your practice.

When I took a look back at my first business plan, I realized I had a very clear understanding of my unique attributes that would contribute to the success of my business. I arrived in my industry with a lot of experience and capability in terms of networking. I was skilled at creating strong partnerships with others, and I leveraged this expertise.

I encourage you to embrace the unique gifts you possess and use them to support your business growth.

Your competitive advantage. The second major section of your business plan focuses on your marketplace, and it is going to be the result of research that you have done. Ideally, you were able to meet with other business owners in your industry and effectively gather information from them to utilize here. This section should address why the market needs your services. Leverage online resources and look at the competitors in your area. Again, look at an approximate 10 or 15-mile radius from where you are planning to practice. Write down some of the strengths and weaknesses of these businesses, as well as their offerings and their pricing. Then define how and why your business will be better than your competitors, and what you're going to do to make your business stand out. This is commonly referred to as your competitive advantage.

Again, looking back at my very first business plan, I noticed that I understood my competitive advantage very well. One of the things I had outlined included orchestrating a client experience that was above and beyond what any other practitioner in my marketplace was doing. This competitive advantage allowed me to charge a premium price in my marketplace early on, even though my business was relatively new.

I will address how I created a superior client experience in the next chapter.

Income and expenses. The third section of the business plan will incorporate sales and expenses. You want to document the following:

- The kind of services you will offer
- The price you will charge for your services
- The products you will offer
- Other income from sources such as sublease income or independent contractors

Your expenses will include monthly items such as:

- Rent
- Utilities
- Prorated amounts for annual items such as malpractice insurance

Using these numbers, you can then create an estimated monthly sales and expense forecast. Note how much income you are going to bring in and roughly estimating how much money you will be able to keep each month.

Marketing. The fourth section of the business plan to develop is your marketing approach. You want to spend a lot of time thinking about your ideal client. Consider the following:

- Who are they?
- Who will appreciate and obtain the greatest value from your competitive advantage?
- How can you attract them to your business?
- Which marketing channels (direct mail, social media, email campaigns) are you going to use to reach them?
- Are you going to provide advertising to them via direct mail?
- Will you use social media to reach them?

As you consider ways to attract new clients when you are just starting out, remember tactics that will keep these customers while continuing to attract more of your ideal clients over time.

When I looked back at the business plan I wrote, I saw that this was an area where I could have done much better. I had talked about my ideal client, but I had not identified them in detail. As a result, many of my marketing efforts resembled throwing things at the wall to see what would stick.

Looking back, I realize that this created a situation where I did a lot of discount pricing in the first six months of my business – something that I see over and over again in our industry. When you fully define your ideal client, craft a compelling message that highlights your competitive advantage, and target your ideal client through the right marketing channels, price discounting is not needed.

Financials. The fifth section of a business plan you need to develop is your financial projections. If you did a good job interviewing other business owners, you have a great foundation.

Here you want to document what your startup costs will be; these will be your initial investments in the business. For example, it could be equipment or supplies you need or a license you have to obtain.

You will want to document your monthly expenses including rent, utilities, and the salary you will pay yourself. Of course, you want to evaluate your forecasted sales in relation to your monthly expenses to make sure that you will break even or ideally make a profit each month.

If you haven't already met with a business mentor to review your initial ideas, now is the time. After you have drafted your business plan, it will be critical for you to find a trusted adviser who can evaluate it. He or she will provide another set of eyes on the goals and ideas that you have laid out for your business. It's also an opportunity for you to communicate your process verbally to another person and receive feedback. When you can have a business mentor review your plan, and you have the opportunity to communicate it verbally, you increase your probability of success.

I associate putting together a business plan with dating. Here's why: Early on when you write a business plan, you invest time on a regular basis to build an intimate relationship with your business. What often happens is that once you think you have learned everything there is to learn (like what might happen in a marriage), you stop "dating." This is an error a lot of holistic practitioners make. You need to continue to date your business. A business plan isn't a one-time thing. It's a fluid document that will expand and contract as you grow and change. I recommend to the business owners I advise to revisit their business plan every three months. Plan a date night!

Business planning is a process. It's documenting a series of actions you are going to take to produce results or reactions. As such, we will continue to talk about all of these areas of your business in the upcoming chapters. If I haven't convinced you at this point that you need a business plan, then starting or growing a business may not be the right next step for you.

Chapter 5

An Experience to Remember

"You earn your clients' loyalty and keep it by continually delivering authentic interactions with you and your business."

Standing out from your competition day after day is a competitive advantage, and when you do that, you no longer need to compete on price. It is well researched and documented that one way to stand out and drive loyalty is by delivering an unforgettable client experience, and that requires a consistent, repeatable process.

This is not a new idea in business. You can see this concept in brands like Apple, Lexus, Disney, and Starbucks. In recent years, even hospitals and financial institutions have begun hiring client loyalty experts. However, you rarely see the owner of a small business focus on loyalty, and you hardly ever see a holistic practitioner do so. But it costs far less to keep a customer than it does to find a new one.

As a practitioner, you focus on delivering your modality with expert care and providing results for your clients. But do you ever take the time to think beyond the one-to-one interaction and look at the overall experience you provide with your business? It will positively influence your clients' perceptions if you deliver consistent value to them day in and day out, not just in the treatment room but throughout every interaction with your business.

ACTION INTO PRACTICE

Visit a place of business you admire and love. What makes it memorable for you?

WHY CREATE AN EXPERIENCE?

We are over-exposed to marketing messages on a daily basis, whether we're surfing the Internet on our phones or computers, watching television, listening to the radio, driving by a billboard, opening our mail, or even talking to friends and family. Most of this information goes in one ear and out the other.

You make your brand stick by delivering an unforgettable "wow" experience. These are the moments that get stored in the long-term memory. Dr. Karl Pribram, neurosurgeon and pioneer in neurobehavioral science, states as a rule of thumb: "We remember 10% of what we read, 20% of what we hear, 30% of what we see, 40% of what we do, and 100% of what we feel."

Unforgettable experiences make an especially strong impact if you provide them consistently while maintaining a high quality of service. Let me provide an example.

I love a cup of quality coffee, and the first time I visited a Starbucks, I was quite enamored – enough so that I went back a second and a third time. At some point, I noticed that I had been visiting several different Starbucks locations, but the coffee was always the same. The experience was also the same. From the moment I walked in the door, I could smell the rich aroma. It was always a relaxing environment because each location was painted in the same earth tones. And I could always find a cozy sofa or chair to sit back and relax in.

Eventually, I began to seek out Starbucks. I would walk further in the airport to get my cup of coffee there. I would drive further to go to one of their locations. They had earned my loyalty by providing a memorable and consistent experience. They influenced my perceptions. They instilled in me a positive attitude about their company. They had earned my loyalty, which resulted in adapting my behavior to make Starbucks my coffeehouse of choice.

As a business owner, you need to influence and activate loyal behavior from your clients.

Different Categories of Clients

From a client engagement perspective, your current clients can be classified as loyal to your business, indifferent, or at-risk. The clients who are at-risk don't have one positive belief or attitude about you. They are price shoppers, and they are easily swayed by special offers. It's likely that they are currently shopping around for another practitioner.

The clients who are indifferent to your business are not necessarily shopping around. But they are price-sensitive, and if you decide to raise your price, they will likely begin seeking other options. They are certainly going to leave if something goes wrong, and they are probably going to be stolen away by another practitioner who delivers an unmatched experience.

The loyal clients will say, stay, and buy. These are your raving fans. They tell their friends and family about you. They don't just want to buy one thing from you; they want to buy all the products and services you offer. And if you make an error, they will probably let you know, but they're not going to leave.

ACTION INTO PRACTICE

In which category are your current clients?

a. At-risk

b. Indifferent

c. Loyal

When I was growing up, my mom worked at a credit union. Therefore, my parents had their accounts there. When I opened my first account, it made perfect sense that I would do so at the same place. Then when I was about 16, I wanted to begin establishing credit, so I thought it would be a good idea to open a credit card. Where did I go? Of course, I went to the trusted credit union where I had a relationship. They issued me a student Visa® card with a line of credit for $200. After college, I was ready to secure my first car loan, and again I went to the trusted credit union *where I had a relationship. They made it a seamless and easy process based on our previous relationship.*

About 10 years later, I was a little frustrated when I was looking to buy my first home. I wanted to go to my trusted credit union to secure the mortgage. Unfortunately, since they were a local business, and I had moved out of state, they couldn't grant me one. But I remained loyal.

Fast forward another 10 years, when I was back in my home state and ready to open my first business. Where did I go? I went to my trusted credit union. I quickly learned that most credit unions are not strongly equipped to support small business owners. Then my loyalty began to fade. I had to look around and find another financial institution that could support me in my business growth. When I did, they were uniquely positioned to deliver an unmatched experience.

Initially, I was loyal to the credit union. But over time, the relationship fizzled, and I moved into a stage of indifference. When I was in a time of need as a business owner, another financial institution was able to swoop in. Not only could the new financial institution provide me with the products and services I needed and desired, but they also took the time to get to know me. They learned my name and welcomed me every time I went in. They also introduced me around the bank. Eventually, they earned my loyalty, and I moved all of my accounts there. And now I recommend them to other small business owners.

That last part is critical; not only have they secured my business, but they have also gained a client who will actively refer new business to them. Such clients will make the difference in your level of success.

Loyalty drives behavior. As business owners, these are the types of behaviors you want to earn and reinforce in your clients.

MAKE IT AN EXPERIENCE

Don't make the error of equating an unforgettable experience with just good customer service. As a practitioner, you need to provide excellent care and service for your clients. You need to do this effectively and in a timely manner. But this is not enough. As a business owner, you must also help your customers to develop an emotional connection with your brand. Your clients want to feel welcomed when they come to your place of business. They want to feel inspired, at ease, and as if you're giving them a big hug. They want to feel loved; they want to feel as if they are coming home.

It is about establishing an emotional connection, and you do that by delivering a consistent experience that incorporates the five senses – sight, touch, taste, smell, and sound. This is a foundational component to creating a memorable client experience that drives loyalty because our senses are a powerful contributor to our memories.

ACTION INTO PRACTICE

How do you currently incorporate the five senses in to your practice?

Our senses are so powerful that when I hear a Rolling Stones song on the radio, I am immediately transported back to the summer when I was 15 years old, had my first job, and was commuting with my dad in the car every day to work. Our senses are so powerful that, when my husband gets near the smell or taste of cheesecake, he is immediately brought back to the time when he had food poisoning as a child because of some cheesecake he ate. Our memories are so powerful that the smell of a specific cologne doesn't just remind me of my husband, but it takes me back to a time when we were dating in college, and he made me dinner at his house for Valentine's Day.

Our senses create emotional memories. As a business owner, you want to tap into that emotional connection with your brand because when you are able to do so, you earn client loyalty.

Here are some examples of how I played to the five senses in my clinic:

- The brand of my business was created to be strong and recognizable using a color associated with trust.
- The name of my business was derived from a personal and memorable story.
- The location of my clinic was intentionally chosen to be off the beaten path. It wasn't in the trendiest location, but it was easily accessible on and off the highway. It had a lot of parking, and the parking was free.
- The building was brand new. It was situated in a natural and serene setting, and it had clear signage.
- There was signage that welcomed our clients when they entered the clinic.

- When a client would come in, someone on our team would greet them and offer them a cup of tea.
- The color palette for the interior of the clinic was carefully selected. It wasn't necessarily my favorite color choice, but I chose it to ensure it elicited a calm, relaxing response from anyone who visited.
- The lighting was selected on purpose. There was no fluorescent lighting, even though it was a commercial building because it was meant to feel like you were coming to a home, not an office.
- There was always classical guitar music playing.
- We diffused essential oils into the air. You could even smell them coming down the hallway before you entered the clinic.
- Our restroom was sparkling clean.
- The décor was minimal, and there were not a lot of product or informational distractions.

These are not haphazard choices. I considered every touch point because I wanted to create an experience for our clients. I wanted people to arrive at the clinic in a setting that reflected a wellness atmosphere. I wanted it to be in a location they could easily find, without driving concerns or parking frustrations. I wanted clients to have a positive-smelling atmosphere when they walked in, one free of musty odors or any lunch smells coming from other tenants in the building. I wanted them to feel welcomed and relaxed from the moment they sat down, prior to them seeing their practitioner.

The objective is to orchestrate an unmatched experience from the first touch points by using the five senses to connect emotionally with your clients. But there are many other touch points to consider as well. You need to think about not just your clients' first interactions with your business but also all subsequent interactions. Consider, for example, the following:

- How will you follow up with your clients after their first visit to your clinic?
- How will you follow up after the second or third visit?
- Will you connect with them on their birthday?
- Will you reconnect with them after a year?
- Will you thank them for the referrals they send?
- How will you handle an unhappy client?

These are all processes that you need to consider how to orchestrate. Not only do these interactions need to be positive, but they also need to be consistent. You earn your clients' loyalty early on and keep it by continually delivering authentic interactions with you and your business.

CHAPTER 6

BIRTH CONTROL FOR YOUR BUSINESS

"Lasting success in business is determined by the processes."

Everything in our lives can be considered a process. Think about your daily routine. When you get up in the morning, do you first get a cup of coffee or jump in the shower? When you get dressed, do you put on your socks before or after you put on your pants? And when you brush your teeth, how much and what kind of toothpaste do you use? Do you floss every day? All of the day-to-day activities such as your morning routine can be broken down and documented as processes.

The same is true for your business. Developing the skills to identify and effectively communicate the processes of how things are accomplished in your business is a critical success factor. It's a skill you can develop, and if you want lasting success in your business, you need to become intimate with the day-to-day processes of your holistic practice.

You may recall I hired my business mentors around the one-year mark. The first thing they recommended was to document the day-to-day operations of my business. They said that I would not be able to grow at the rate I was anticipating and projecting without this documentation.

Now I can share with you how it was a critical success factor for me. It allowed for ease in the hiring and training of employees, and it empowered my decision-making. I have never regretted documenting the day-to-day processes of my business; in fact, I wish I had written down things sooner. I also found that every time I would go back and refer to this documentation, I wished I had included even greater detail.

BUSINESS OPERATIONS

Business operations are the activities involved in the day-to-day functions of your business. You may not have realized it, but we have already talked about quite a few areas of your business where the processes are critical.

First, we discussed having people on your team who are your everyday "peeps." These are people who you hire and fire. They could be individuals who work for your business as independent contractors. Most of us will interact with someone like this at some point. If you do, have you considered what process you will use? For example, what is your process when you hire or fire people? If you won't have employees per se, but you will sublease your space or hire independent contractors, have you thought about how and what process you will use to onboard them into your business?

This was a critical part of my business plan. Over the years, my clinic had a mix of employees and independent contractors. I also sublet some of my space. For that reason, developing a detailed onboarding process for my business was a necessity. It took a while, but over time I was able to put together a distinct four-week timeline that we used to onboard practitioners. It started with an information sheet we provided the practitioner at our initial meeting with them. It was a way to highlight everything our clinic would be able to help them with, such as administrative and marketing support.

ACTION INTO PRACTICE

Additional areas to create process in your business operations:

- *Unplanned time out of the office*
- *Weather*
- *Scheduling*

Then we had a very detailed checklist of things we needed to discuss with the practitioner before we signed a contract with them. We did this because we knew that once we had executed a contract, we would be investing a lot of time in this practitioner. Among other things, we would set them up for access to the building, provide them with log-ins, create a business card for them, and set them up in our scheduling and billing system. Before moving on to this stage, we wanted to be certain we had a wonderfully executed contract and a passionate practitioner. We also wanted to make sure that we had discussed any potential hurdles that could come up later.

Once this stage was complete, we identified that we wanted to communicate the same information about our policies and procedures to everyone. We put together a procedures manual, and we reviewed it with every new team member who came into our office during the in-office orientation. It was an opportunity to go over the policies and procedures as well as collect forms and have an initial marketing meeting kick-off.

I share this with you to show you how we created a detailed process for the onboarding. It was a repeatable process that helped ensure we didn't miss anything. It also allowed us to provide everyone the same information, and it lessened the risk of us over-investing our resources before we had a firm commitment with each practitioner. The roles were made extremely clear, so we knew who on our team was responsible at each stage. Finally, although it was not the main goal of this process, it was our first opportunity to provide a high level of professionalism with our practitioners and an opportunity for us to model the behavior we wanted them to exhibit with our brand.

BUSINESS PLANNING

The next area to look at with regards to processes is business planning. Hopefully, Chapter 4 helped you to understand the importance of writing a business plan and reviewing it every three months.

ACTION INTO PRACTICE

Select and place into your calendar the dates you will review your business plan this year.

Early on, I made an error regarding my business planning process. When I graduated from school, I did write a business plan. It was the first thing I began doing before I even started my business. The one thing I didn't do was check back. I didn't keep a regular "date" with my business plan. That was my error.

The upside was that I had a well thought-out business plan, which I executed successfully, even exceeding my projections in the first six months. However, my plans weren't big enough. By six months, the business had so much momentum that I had surpassed my original plan and no longer had a plan in place for where my business was going. Things were coming at me so quickly that I was saying "yes" to everything instead of strategically saying "yes" to what I was working toward. Since I didn't have a plan anymore, I didn't know what I was working toward or where I was heading. And since I hadn't been "dating" and updating my business plan, I had to slow down so that I could speed up again.

Client Experience

The third area where processes play a critical role in your success is the client experience. We talked about defining the touch points with your clients to make a repeatable process that is easy to communicate to your team. But it's also important to define the customer service aspects of the client experience.

One part of the client experience I completely missed in the beginning was identifying how to handle clients when they were unhappy after an interaction with my business.

When I first started, it was just me and another practitioner, so I didn't think about handling dissatisfaction. To be honest, in one and a half years, we didn't have any unhappy clients, so it didn't cross my mind how I might handle them.

As the practice grew —as we added more team members and more clients were coming through on a day-to-day basis, there were more opportunities for oversights or somebody to be unhappy. It was a great opportunity to develop a training process for my team. The training process would communicate clearly what type of client experience we were delivering and how we were delivering it. It was also an opportunity to create a process around how we would handle an unhappy client. It can happen to anyone, and it happened to me. Somebody became very unhappy; we didn't have a clear process on how to handle it, and we lost the client.

ACTION INTO PRACTICE

Outline the first three steps you will take when handling an unhappy client.

You can do a lot of things right most of the time, but expecting everything will go right all of the time is unrealistic. That is why having processes around your day-to-day operations is critical.

These are some examples of the areas where defining and documenting processes and procedures for your business will set you up for lasting success. We will continue talking about it in the upcoming sections because it applies to everything in the day-to-day function of your business. It applies to your practices in sales, marketing, and accounting.

Benefits of Documentation

It is best to look at operations and documentation early on. Below are some of the benefits of doing so.

It will save you time. Time is extremely precious for a business owner. As your practice grows, you'll find that the competition for your time becomes greater and greater, and the complexity of your business will undoubtedly become greater and greater as well. If you can take a look at what you're doing, get it down on paper, and revisit it on a regular basis, you'll be able to add more as you go along. This is much easier than looking at it several years down the road and trying to remember everything.

It allows you to understand the "why." When you look at your processes, procedures, and what you're doing, you also have an opportunity to understand the "why." As a business owner, understanding the "why" is critical. Understanding why you do things ensures you have a great depth of understanding of your business. It also makes sure that you stay focused on the right things. And as a busy business owner, staying focused is vital.

It positions you for growth. Mapping out your processes and procedures will position you for growth. As I mentioned previously, at one stage, I had to slow down so I could speed up. If I had taken the time to check back on my business plan, it would have allowed me to progress with much greater momentum. It's important to take the time to do the less glamorous tasks so you are positioned for growth and can seize opportunities when they arrive at your doorstep.

It helps define roles. Documenting operations also allows you to define the roles in your business clearly. This reinforces positioning your business for growth. If you have documented all the day-to-day functions of your business, it's a great help when you're ready to hire someone. For example, say you're ready to outsource your bookkeeping. Documentation allows you to know exactly what you have been doing, how you're doing it, and why you're doing it. This streamlines your ability to outsource the role to someone else because it's very clearly defined by you.

It ensures consistency. Documentation ensures activities are consistently done. Maybe you don't outsource a task, but you communicate it to another practitioner or employee. Then you can take the information you already have about what you're doing, why you're doing it, and how you're doing it, and you can hand it off to someone. Because you have a set of procedures, they can consistently duplicate what you have done, and that empowers others on your team to execute effectively without relying on you 100 percent of the time.

ACTION INTO PRACTICE

Make a list of processes within your practice that you can document. Set aside 30 minutes each week to work on this list.

It reduces your risk. Finally, and most importantly, the reason documenting processes and procedures is so critical for you as a business owner is that it prepares you for the unexpected. When you're a business owner, the day-to-day function of your business solely relies on you. If something happens, and you're not prepared – you do not have a Plan B or a backup in case of an emergency – it will be a critical time for you. It places your business and all you have built at risk.

To establish a solid foundation for success, it is best to look at your processes early on and document them. You also want to identify the person who could pick up your responsibilities in the event you're not able to fulfill them. Even if you are the only one in your business, you still need a system for everything ranging from who is going to pay your bills to how to follow up with your clients. If you have a bigger team, then who will make sure payroll is taken care of? These are all critical elements of running a business.

Clarity, consistency, outsourcing, and worst-case scenarios are the main reasons why it's important to take a look at your processes early on in your business and continue to add to and re-evaluate them. Lasting success in business is determined by the processes. Having a greater understanding and documentation of the day-to-day operations of your business is like built-in business protection. That's why I call it birth control for your business.

Everything you do on a daily basis is a series of actions, and these actions produce outcomes. Clearly defining, documenting, and communicating all of these actions are skills you want to practice regularly and refine over time. As a business owner, mastering these principles will almost guarantee your outcomes will be positive, and it will position you for growth.

SECTION 3

PROFITABILITY

Chapter 7

Aligning Your Talents with People Who Desire Them

"Align the client needs and desires in your market with what your holistic practice has to offer that is uniquely different."

We all need to make money to support ourselves, contribute to our families, pay off our student loans, travel, or pay for whatever else we desire. To have the income you require, you need your business to be profitable or else you just have an expensive hobby.

In this section, we will examine how focusing your marketing efforts will provide accelerated results for your practice. Then we will consider why you don't necessarily need to be selling, but you do need to develop a sales process. Lastly, we will discuss the importance of tracking and evaluating the numbers.

THE BASICS

You don't have to be an expert on marketing to ensure your holistic practice is a success, but you need to have a good understanding of the basics. The simple definition of marketing is the ability to identify and satisfy a need in the marketplace, and to do this for profit. It involves using research to understand and focus on what the client wants and desires. It's not necessarily about what you have to offer but about what the client desires. It's about filling an unmet need in your marketplace.

Next, you need to put together a strategy for how you will fulfill these desires. You want to develop the strategy based on your defined competitive advantage or point of differentiation. Then you choose a segment of the marketplace, or an ideal client, who wants what you have to offer. The strategy should take the following into consideration:

- The services you're going to offer
- Any complementary products you will offer
- How you will price these products and services, or if you will package them together
- What channels you will use to promote them

When you put together your strategy, you want to consider whether or not you will need any additional resources, products, or team members. Let me provide an example.

There used to be an all-natural and organic retail store in the same area as my clinic. They offered skincare products and makeup as well as facial and anti-aging services for this marketplace. At that time, we didn't offer many anti-aging treatments. We only offered facial rejuvenation acupuncture.

When the retail store closed, I believed there to be an opportunity to fulfill an unmet need in my geographical area. I also thought my clinic was uniquely positioned to capture part of this marketplace because we were a boutique clinic, and we offered our clients a very high-end experience. We also offered holistic and natural solutions in healthcare.

I saw an opportunity for my clinic to capture some of this marketplace, so I decided to repackage what we already had. I combined the facial rejuvenation acupuncture with infrared sauna sessions and organic skin care solutions, both of which we already offered. Then I added facials. Offering the facials required that I hired an esthetician. I also increased the breadth of my organic skincare line.

The original anti-aging offerings that I had in my clinic were very unfocused. I had no strategy built around them. What I developed was a focused strategy that met a market demand – the people in my geographical marketplace already wanted these offerings. It leveraged my competitive advantage, which was that we were a high-end clinic. Many practitioners are afraid to be as specific as this, but the more specific you can be, the better.

Identifying Your Competitive Advantage

As a holistic practitioner, identifying and leveraging what makes you special and unique is the beginning of creating a targeted marketing plan that drives more of the right clients to your practice. What is your competitive advantage? Why are people going to drive further to see you? Why are they going to pay more, come back, and refer all of their family and friends? Here are several questions you can ask yourself to begin identifying what makes you special:

- Do you have any special training?
- Have you been in the marketplace longer than anyone else or seen more clients?
- Do you have well-documented results of treating a specific condition?
- Do you have a special degree or combination of education and experience?

When you begin to ask yourself these types of questions, you will begin to uncover what elements of your competitive advantage serve your marketplace.

Once you have determined what sets you apart, you want to begin shouting it from the hilltops. Tell everyone about what makes you stand out, and use it in every marketing channel you leverage.

When you think about what makes you fabulous, and you want to communicate it to the marketplace, it is extremely helpful to communicate it in a one or two-sentence format. In general, it should be something along the lines of, "(practitioner or clinic name) is the best at (one or two things), because of (list

ACTION INTO PRACTICE

List two unique talents you offer to your clients as a healer.

one or two things)." This is often referred to as an "elevator pitch" because its brevity allows it to be shared during a quick elevator ride.

One example of competitive advantage is a practitioner who offers athletic performance and synergy solutions by combining their expertise as a personal trainer, massage therapist, and acupuncturist.

Another example of competitive advantage is a community acupuncture clinic that provides the most experienced staff at the best price. They have been serving their city since 2000 and have completed over 10,000 client visits starting at only $15.

Even if you are the only practitioner of your kind in your marketplace, you still need a competitive advantage. It could be that you are the city's most trusted and valued practitioner serving men, women, and children in their primary health care needs with up-to-date and cutting-edge therapeutic techniques.

This would be a great statement because if you are the only practitioner in a marketplace, and you can serve the entire family, this is essential information. It also reassures potential clients that you stay up-to-date and relevant, which is another important factor.

Your Ideal Client

Once you have developed your message, you want to begin creating a story or a picture of the ideal client for what you offer. Then you will decide what channels you want to use to reach them.

> **ACTION INTO PRACTICE**
>
> *Write a one-page story about your ideal client.*

Create an image of who your perfect client is and begin to write a story about them. You may include some demographic information, but your story should be a more detailed picture of a day in their life. What do they like and dislike? What are their biggest dreams? What are their daily challenges? What is their greatest fear? You want to be as specific as possible.

As an example, let's look at the ideal client for a practitioner who offers athletic performance and synergy solutions, which was the first competitive advantage example I provided.

This ideal client might be someone named Colleen. Colleen is 50 years old, and her children are grown. All her life, she has been an enthusiast of everything sports-related. She is currently working out at the gym three or four times a week doing weightlifting, and she is also a runner. She considers going to the gym a hobby, and most of her friends and social connections hang out at her gym. She is extremely concerned with staying fit as she ages, and she wants to maintain her strength, her flexibility, and her cardiovascular health. She loves group fitness classes and loves education regarding fitness.

Diet is also extremely important to Colleen. She shops for organic food and takes supplements on a daily basis. She has a fear of getting older and her body failing her. She owns her own home, drives a Volkswagen, and has a dog.

This is an example of being very specific and telling a story about the exact individual who would want what you offer.

Marketing Channels

Once you have identified your ideal client clearly, you will be better equipped to select the appropriate marketing channels to reach them.

Action into Practice

Name three marketing channels that are best to reach your ideal client.

There are a lot of different opportunities and channels available to you. One approach is to focus on public relations, doing news releases, or writing articles for local papers. Another option is to focus on leveraging events, such as webinars, doing speaking engagements, or attending conferences and trade shows. You could also network by sitting on the board of directors of an organization or attending meetings of your local Chamber of Commerce. In addition, you can utilize the online social media channels such as Facebook, Instagram, or Twitter. Online, you can also use search engine optimization (SEO) and run banner advertisements. Then there are offline media opportunities such as TV, radio, or print advertising. Referrals are also considered a marketing channel. Here you leverage word-of-mouth or affiliate relationships.

As the owner of a business, it can be quite overwhelming to have all these options for marketing. When you first identify who you are trying to attract to your business, you are better equipped to select suitable channels.

Begin with the two or three channels that will present the best opportunity for you to interact with your ideal client and capture their attention. You want to think about how they spend their time, where they hang out, and what they do outside of work. Then select the marketing channels that best position you to reach them.

If we stay with our example of Colleen and remember what is important to her, we're better able to select the channels to find her. Colleen hangs out at the gym, so the best place to spend your time networking would be at gyms. Perhaps you can connect with other business owners who run or operate these facilities. Colleen also likes to shop for organic food, and she purchases supplements. If you wanted speaking opportunities, then a co-op or a store selling natural foods or supplements would be a great place to approach to find your ideal client. If you wanted to do some writing, you could look for opportunities on sports-related blogs, in a magazine exclusively for runners, or even in a running club. When targeting someone like Colleen, with search engine optimization (SEO) for your website, you wouldn't just want to use keywords for the modalities you offer. You would also want to optimize the site for sports-related terms.

Once you understand the client needs and desires in your market, it is extremely important to know what your holistic practice has to offer that is uniquely different. This will help you understand who your ideal client is and select the marketing channels where you can reach them. This brings focus to your marketing efforts versus trying to throw things at the wall to see what will stick. As a result, if you are consistent in your efforts, you will increase and accelerate your business growth.

Allocating Time

The last step I want to mention regarding marketing is to create and designate times specifically to work on these marketing strategies. This is a step that many business owners miss.

Designate a specific time on your calendar every week for marketing related activities and put together a marketing calendar for the year. This way, you ensure that you not only get it done but also deliver content consistently.

Let's wrap up with our example of Colleen. If you want to network with gyms in your local area, and you have found five gyms, you will approach one per week for the next five weeks. To set up speaking events at local co-ops and supplement stores, make a list of these stores, and then approach all of them over the next four weeks. Your goal will be to have one speaking event per month throughout the year. If you want to write some articles or other content for sports-related blogs, then you will make a list of these

> **Action into Practice**
>
> *Block time each week on your calendar to dedicate to marketing-related activities.*

blogs, and approach one of them every two weeks over the next four weeks. These are some examples of how to schedule your marketing efforts.

CHAPTER 8

YOUR WAKE-UP CALL

"Without clients coming in the door, you cannot be a practitioner and heal people."

The word sales can have negative connotations. Sometimes when I hear that word, it conjures up images of people who sell used cars or those people at the kiosks in the malls who always try to push their products on you.

It's hard for me to believe that I was in sales for 15 years because it was not my most likely career choice. But what I learned during this time was invaluable; I learned that sales is not about selling. I realized that it's more about aligning what clients want with what you have to offer and understanding the process they need to go through in their buying decisions. The role of selling is about your ability to lead them through that process.

This is why sales is much more about the process than actual selling. When you have a targeted and planned marketing strategy and clear sales process, you become unstoppable. In my experience, holistic practitioners struggle not only with getting new clients in the door but also with earning their repeat business. Remember, it costs far more to secure a new client than to keep an existing one. Therefore, keeping the clients you have, and getting them to refer you is the key to a successful business.

GETTING NEW CLIENTS

Practitioners struggle with getting new clients for one of two reasons. Either they don't have any marketing activities in place, or they are doing lots of marketing activities that lack focus.

Let's talk first about those of you who have little to no marketing activity in place. As a business owner, you have many different roles to fulfill. When you choose to become a business owner, you choose to be in sales by default. Here is your "wake-up call": You can't just show up at your practice every day and hope that clients will emerge because hope is not a strategy.

Most of you define yourselves solely as practitioners and see yourselves as a healer in your field. You need to undo this way of thinking. Instead, embrace a self-view that says, "I am a business owner. I have many jobs in my business, and my number one job is sales." Without clients coming in the door, you cannot be a practitioner and heal people.

Over time, I have worked with many different practitioners in my clinic, and I have come to see two distinct approaches to building a business. One type of practitioner would come in during their contracted hours. Early on, as with all of us, they didn't have a full schedule of clients coming in. These practitioners would come into the clinic each day, and they would sit and wait to see if anyone would call or show up at the door seeking a same-day service. While they were waiting, they would study to become more of an expert in their field.

By contrast, I had other practitioners who had a very different approach. Knowing that their schedule wasn't going to be full early on, they would schedule networking meetings in those unfilled hours. Sometimes they would come into the office to send e-mails to former clients or contact friends and family about their new position. They would even post special offers on social media. Hopefully, I don't have to tell you who had the greatest success.

> **Action into Practice**
>
> *Do you have too little time dedicated to marketing, or do you have too many activities that are unfocused?*

As a practitioner, you have already spent years becoming an expert. You don't need to spend any additional time on that. Your success is going to come from focusing your efforts on marketing and sales. If your business doesn't have clients, you are soon out of business.

Now, let's further discuss those who are out doing marketing activities that lack focus. Those of you in this situation talk about being run down and exhausted. You are doing a lot of things, and you have an income, but the income is not as large as you desire.

The great news is that you understand the need to be out working in your sales role within your business and exposing yourself and your business to others in the community. The problem is that your efforts are unfocused and not producing the results you desire.

A practitioner like this writes articles and blogs, sends out information via e-mail marketing, posts on Facebook, is involved in their local Chamber of Commerce, and volunteers in their local community. All of these are activities for driving business in the door. But the amount of input they generate does not equal the output or revenue they want.

A practitioner, Sue, came to me and said that she was passionate about working with women before, during, and after their pregnancy. I asked Sue what type of marketing activities and sales activities she was doing and whether or not she was networking. She was both networking and writing. After further discussion, we discovered she was doing a lot of great sales focused activities that she enjoyed and leveraged her strengths, but they were not focused on pregnant women – her ideal client!

THE SALES PROCESS

The bad news for some of you is that as a business owner, you are first and foremost in sales, and you need to accept that. The good news is that you don't need to sell at all. You simply need to have a very clear focus and develop a process.

We began the discussion of focus in the last chapter, and we're going to build on it now because every practitioner has unique talents as a healer that must be leveraged. You have a combination of knowledge and expertise that makes you special. For example, some practitioners arrive with a unique combination of education. Others may have a unique position because of their experiences.

Knowing your competitive advantage allows you to define your ideal clients and determine the two or three top channels you will use to reach these clients. This is the beginning of a focused process. You have the knowledge and the expertise, and you align it with the ideal client and the appropriate channels.

Action into Practice

What solutions do you currently offer your clients?

Next, you want to bring in the offer. A lot of holistic practitioners make an error here. At this stage, you do not want to talk about your services. You're not offering a massage, acupuncture, or naturopathic medicine. You offer solutions backed by a unique experience.

The practitioner mentioned before, Sue, who was passionate about working with pregnant women, doesn't offer services; she offers relief from nausea and heartburn during pregnancy. She offers natural pain management during labor. She might even offer decreased recovery time from C-sections.

You have your knowledge and expertise. You know who your ideal client is and the channels you will use to reach them, and now you will offer them solutions – not services. This will allow you to earn their business. This is the segment of sales you might think of as conversion or closing the deal.

Potential client opportunities will arrive in your practice in many different forms. You might get a phone call from a networking event that you attended. You may have someone schedule a free consultation if you offer that. Or someone might even book an initial visit with you. It doesn't matter if they just call for an inquiry, or if they have chosen to schedule an appointment with you. You need to think about them all in the same way because they are not yet your loyal fans.

For each of these interactions, you need to think about bringing the potential client or the first time client through a process. This process will have some key elements.

You want to make sure you take the opportunity to make a connection with them and spend some time being personable and building rapport before you move into the assessment.

Then you want to take time to uncover what they want and desire. In your interaction with them, you want to share some of your knowledge and expertise, and your past results. But you do not want to use this time to talk about your services or what you provide as a modality. You want to talk about the solution. Match what they want with the solutions you can offer.

Thinking about each client interaction in terms of the process lays the foundation for "closing the sale" and earning repeat business. This is the next area where many practitioners struggle. If you take the time to attract your ideal clients, you get to know them, and you do not offer them a service but instead a solution, then you have already laid a beautiful groundwork to earn repeat business. The key is how you follow up with them and the experience you orchestrate and deliver to them on a consistent basis.

Hopefully, at this stage, you see how it is all about the process and how one area of your business flows seamlessly into the other. The one key area that we haven't talked about yet is the need to create a funnel of new clients for your business. We will discuss this in the next chapter.

Chapter 9

Show Up and Show Off

"Potential clients make the decision to work with you solely based on how you appear online compared to your competition."

The first time that I used social media was back when I was still working in corporate America. I ended up creating a LinkedIn profile because I found that some of my connections were using it as a place to manage their contacts online. We would connect there occasionally, but I didn't spend a lot of time on it. The same was true with Facebook; I had a personal profile, but I didn't spend much time there. I just used it as a place to keep track of and touch base with some of my friends and family back home.

When I started my first business, I wasn't thinking much about social media and how I might leverage it. But at the urging of people around me, I did decide, very early on, to put up a Facebook page for my business, and I also set up a Twitter account. As a new business owner, it still didn't seem extremely important to me. I had many new tasks, and since I was feeling quite overwhelmed, it wasn't something I considered a priority. I can tell you, I was wrong!

Social media is an extremely powerful tool to gain social proof for your business very early on. You can use it to attract leads, gain visibility, drive traffic to your website, and engage and gather feedback from your audience. I am by no means the expert, but I have become an active user and have firsthand experience with its benefits in terms of growing a business. I feel so strongly about its importance for the success of your holistic practice that I wanted to include a chapter to at least get you started.

ACTION INTO PRACTICE

Search online for your name and/or business name. What are you able to learn?

SOCIAL PROOF

Most people are online every day, whether it's on a computer at work or their phones in their spare time. One of the very first things someone will do when they want to find out more about you and potentially make an appointment with you is to check you out online. They might search for your website. They will look for you in major search engines, and they will read about you in individual profiles or business profiles on social media. This is what potential clients today do before they consider working with you. They want the opportunity to get to know you first. That is why social media channels need to be in place.

The social media channels don't just need to be in place; they need to have a very similar look and feel that aligns with your brand. There should be a consistent story across all of the channels you use because this is, first and foremost, social proof that your business exists. It's your first conversation with a potential client. It communicates the type of experience they may expect working with you and the level of professionalism of your business.

Your social media presence is the first impression you give your potential clients. For that reason, you don't just want to show up. I recommend you take the opportunity to show off. It's a valuable asset to look a little bit bigger than you are to begin the process of winning over clients. It's not just about existing; it's about how you exist. Social media creates an opportunity to attract clients. This is why it's so important to show up big and consistently.

Potential clients make the decision to work with you solely based on how you appear online compared to your competition. You may not like it, but it's true!

Let me give you an example. It is quite common for holistic practitioners to leverage some of the local marketing opportunities around them. For instance, many co-ops or coffee and tea shops will have an opportunity or community board where you can post your flyers and your business card.

In this example, there is a woman who finds your card at a local coffee shop. On your card, you happen to have some information about how you specialize in prenatal care, and she is looking for this expertise. After she has had her coffee, she heads back to the office and takes a few moments to look at your website. Unfortunately, she doesn't see anything about prenatal care. She looks a little bit further and tries to find you on Facebook, but you don't have a business page. She finally goes to a major search engine online and enters, "holistic prenatal care practitioners." In this search, you do not come up, but your competition does. She takes a look at their website and finds out they have a lot of information specific to prenatal care. They also have some consistent messaging on their social media page. Instead of calling you, she calls them for an appointment. This happens all too often. You created an opportunity, but unfortunately it was for your competitor.

Social media offers exposure for your business, and much of it is free. There are also paid advertising options that can create a great lead funnel for your business. I highly encourage you to learn about these options and leverage them. However, updating your network on business milestones, sharing some of your success stories, or writing about ways you can help provides you with valuable, free exposure for your business. It can keep you top of mind with your audience.

Gathering Feedback and Creating Engagement

Once your business has a more established presence, you will have a greater opportunity to gain valuable feedback from your audience. For example, say you are thinking about adding a new service or product to your clinic. Instead of immediately moving forward, you may engage your audience on social media and ask them what type of additional products or services they would like to see from you. You can use this as a tool to keep them engaged, not just by asking questions but by polling them and pushing out announcements about events or new initiatives at your clinic.

Choosing Channels

There are many online channels you can use to target these efforts, and it can be difficult to decide which ones to choose.

> **Action into Practice**
>
> *Besides Facebook, what one additional social media channel is best to reach your ideal client?*

First and foremost, you need to consider your ideal client. Then select the top two to three social media channels they frequent. For example, say your ideal clients are stay-at-home moms. Stay-at-home moms are less likely to spend a lot of time on LinkedIn because this is a social media network that leans more heavily towards professional networking for corporate types. Stay-at-home moms are more likely to spend time on Facebook or Pinterest.

Second, I would recommend that every business owner and all practitioners start with Facebook. Five new profiles are added to Facebook every five seconds, and they have around 865 million log-ins on a daily basis. Though this data is probably out of date already, it shows how much Facebook is used, and it reinforces that it is a great place to start.

Finally, I recommend you consider creating a LinkedIn profile for yourself. I have done a lot of networking with other practitioners, business owners, and community leaders in my area. I found they were less likely to search for me on a social network like Facebook and more likely to want to connect with me via LinkedIn. It goes back to what makes the most sense for you and your ideal client.

UTILIZING YOUR CHANNELS

Once you've decided which are the best channels to reach your audience, there are some general tips for utilizing social media that you want to consider.

Cross-link your efforts. If you have a Facebook and LinkedIn page for yourself or your business, you want to make sure you highlight these on your website. If you have a personal Facebook page, you would want to list your business page as one of the places you have worked.

Fill out your profile completely. Remember, when your audience looks you up on Facebook or LinkedIn, it is their first opportunity to find out more about you. You want to give them as much information as you can. Think about it as a way for them to get to know you.

Provide content on a regular basis. You can imagine what it would signify if you set up some social media platforms; leverage them on a daily, weekly, or monthly basis for several months; and then just stop it altogether. Individuals who are interested in working with you could get the impression that you may have gone out of business. So if you use these channels, you want to leverage them on a regular basis.

Don't be overly promotional. People do not respond well to businesses that are sales-y. Instead, you want to provide value. You could add a link to a blog post you have written recently. Another option is to make a short video about your clinic. Or you could even post some behind-the-scenes snapshots that give people an opportunity to get to know you on a more personal level. Most importantly, you want to be yourself.

Quality over quantity is essential. Rather that five daily posts that mean nothing, create one post each day that is extremely targeted and speaks to the types of clients you are trying to attract. You also want to think about high quality, not just content. If you use a photo, for example, developing a high-quality picture with lots of colors is going be a lot more engaging. It is worth spending a little extra time to add a custom look and feel.

ACTION INTO PRACTICE

How effectively are you utilizing your social media channels? What is the first step you will take to improve?

Track your results. This is one of the errors I see a lot of practitioners, and small businesses in general, make. Social media in our context is a business tool. The content is not just something you post on a regular basis with the hope that something sticks. You do it for the purpose of marketing and communicating with your existing and potential ideal clients. You want to find out if that is working for you, and tracking analytics will give you the insight you need.

Build the use of social media into your business plan. You need to be clear on the goals you are trying to achieve using the social media channels. You want to know what you use, why you use it, how you are going to use it, and the results you expect.

I didn't leverage social media early on. Though I had a presence, I still had a very homegrown look and feel to my brand even after one year in business. Then, around year one, I decided to hire someone to help me with branding. They created a more professional look and feel which carried from my website to my Facebook page and my LinkedIn profile. It was very consistent. I also began to put money into search engine optimization and advertising on social media.

The change was like night and day. My phone started ringing, and new leads came into my business without me having to go out and hustle. I am convinced it was a result of the high-end branding effort and leveraging my online presence in a new way.

Social media offers an opportunity for you as a holistic practitioner to provide social proof that your business exists and operates at a professional level. Your ongoing efforts need to be focused on keeping your audience engaged by providing high-quality content, using your audience to gain feedback about current and future decisions for your business, and leveraging it as a tool to attract new clients.

CHAPTER 10

FINANCIAL NUTRITION

"Documenting the details of what is coming in and what is going out enables you to ask educated questions about your business."

As a practitioner, you are interested in knowing what your clients put into their bodies on a day-to-day basis and what is coming out. Your ability to take the time to thoroughly understand the day-to-day habits of your clients and how they treat their bodies plays a great role in their overall treatment and the holistic health plan that you put together for them.

Just like you take great care and concern to look at the entire picture and details of the day-to-day life of your clients, you also need to do the same for your business. It is critical for you as a business owner to understand what is coming into your business in terms of income, what is going out in terms of expenses, and if there is anything left over. It is time to talk about money.

Too many holistic practitioners are struggling to make the amount of money they desire. In my experience, it is a result of practitioners discounting their prices or giving away their services. It is also a result of them focusing only on the money that comes in.

Instead, begin thinking about money in terms of the entire picture. Rather than focusing purely on making a specific salary, look beyond just one number. Look at all the numbers of your business and use that information to evaluate the overall health of your business.

In a way, it's like when clients come to you, and you talk with them and ask them about their nutritional habits. They usually end up saying something like, "Well, I eat pretty well, and I have daily bowel movements, so everything is good with me." As a practitioner, you know that is not enough information to put together a complete picture of your client's health.

The same is true for your business. It's not enough to look at your income only or focus only on how you can pay yourself a specific salary. You need to look at the overall picture and understand the numbers of your business because you are powerless without these details. Without them, you will not be in a position to make informed and effective

> **ACTION INTO PRACTICE**
>
> *How are you currently documenting income and expenses in your practice?*

decisions for your business. With them, you are empowered to make educated decisions for your business.

Bookkeeping

To look at and understand the numbers, you first have to document them. This critical step is one that many practitioners completely avoid. There are several great tools to document your income and expenses. The one that I happen to know best is QuickBooks. It's a software product that allows you to document your sales and track your expenses.

If you don't know anything about accounting or QuickBooks, an organization like SCORE (www.score.org) can help you. They have local chapters in many communities across the US where they offer a free QuickBooks class. Another option is to meet with your trusted adviser your accountant for a couple of hours, and let them set up your bookkeeping system and teach you the basics.

The perfect time to set up a bookkeeping system is at the very beginning of your business. One reason is that you're not very busy. You have more time to get set up and begin to learn how to document and to do basic accounting.

It also provides you an opportunity to document where you started. Over time, you can look at the progression of your business, which will build your confidence. Having the data allows you to analyze your business later on. One very smart business man told me "It's hard to save the first dollar earned if you do not know where it is."

The last reason to set up a bookkeeping system early is that it just makes things easier for you. For example, you are required to track and pay sales and use tax. Believe it or not, I have seen practitioners pull out Excel spreadsheets and handwritten tallies of their reporting for sales and use tax. If you start to use a tool like QuickBooks, it becomes a much less cumbersome process. In QuickBooks, there is a report you run to see what you will be paying on an annual basis or what you need to pay for that quarter, this also allows you to plan ahead.

Two years after I started my business, I wanted to make a large equipment purchase for my practice, and I decided I needed a loan from my financial institution. It was not something I had done before. My financial institution said they needed to see the financial health of my business and wanted specific reports from me. I was extremely thankful I could access the information quickly and present it to them in a professional way.

I have seen many practitioners who are not in the position to provide documentation of their income and expenses. You may not think you need this documentation today, but how will you prepare for annual taxes, and what will you need in one or two years from now?

POWERFUL DECISION-MAKING

Beginning to develop this systematic process for documenting income and expenses of your business is an absolute must, whether you do it yourself or outsource it to a bookkeeper. It is the step beyond this that is exciting for a business owner because now you have information that empowers you and places you in the position to begin evaluating the information. With this information, you can begin to make more powerful decisions for your business.

Every business owner must take the time to learn how to read, understand, and make conclusions about their business using basic financial reports. A tool like QuickBooks will allow you to run very specific financial reporting easily. It could be a balance sheet or profit and loss statement. Do yourself a favor: Make it a goal to learn at least these two reports, and review them on a monthly basis.

Even if you choose to ignore my advice of learning these basic financial reports, there is still a way for you to begin to look at and understand your business. Simply take the information you put in and review a list of your expenses and your list of sales reports.

Expenses. Let's discuss expenses first. As I mentioned, you can run a report. I'm not talking about a report of your total expenses for the year, the quarter, or the month. I'm talking about reviewing a detailed list of all of your expenses.

Let me give you some examples of how you might use this information to your benefit. Say you were planning for next year. Then you want to take a look at your detailed list of expenses by month and year. Which of these expenses were unplanned or unforeseen? By adding up all of these, you will have the dollar amount you will need to build into your budget for the following year to help you plan ahead. Then you will have money ready for these unexpected expenses.

Also look at where you overspent for the year. Where did the numbers look too large, and what expenses could you cut in that area for the upcoming year?

You don't always just have to make more money. There is often an opportunity to reallocate money you spent, or reduce expenses. You can move money to your marketing budget. Or maybe you want to increase your salary, but you don't want to work more hours. This approach allows you to look at your information and leverage your income in different ways.

Another way to look at your expenses that can be very valuable for you as a business owner is to look at where most of your money is going out in a year's time frame. Typically, the top expenses for a business owner will be rent paid to a landlord and wages for themselves or their employees. For example, perhaps your landlord determined that your rent is going up next year, or you want to increase the salary for your employees. Then you need to understand how this will affect your business and determine where the money is going to come from.

These are just a few examples of how you can look at a simple list of expenses and begin to leverage the information to make better decisions for your business.

Income. You can do the same with sales information or the money coming in. Again, you don't just want to look at the total sales. You want to review a more detailed report and ask more questions. It will allow you to make more effective decisions.

For example, look at your income by month. Which months tend to be slower? During which months are most of your business coming in? This will help you identify if there is an ideal time for you to take an extended vacation to minimize the financial impact. Or say you want to take continuing education classes, but you want to minimize the financial impact. By reviewing this information, you are able to determine if there are better times of the year for doing these activities than others.

Another example is to look at your sales by product and service. This information helps you understand the top products being sold in your business and know the number one service that's being purchased. This is powerful information. It tells you what your clients want from your business and where you should be focusing your marketing efforts. In addition, if you are planning to increase your price, you can evaluate the numbers to find out how this will affect your business based on how much of it you are already selling.

Action into Practice

Schedule a reoccurring appointment in your calendar each month to review your income and expenses.

A final example is to begin to evaluate your sales information by customer. This is extremely valuable. Instead of running a report by product or service, take a look at it in descending order of the customer.

For a typical business, a good rule of thumb is 80 percent of sales come from 20 percent of your clients. What is your percentage compared to this? Who are the individuals who are delivering the bulk of your business? Having this knowledge gives you the opportunity to understand where your business has deep relationships. It also allows you to identify the individuals who might be the early adopters of new products and services you are going to launch, and it will help you see who you can approach for referrals.

These are just some of the ways you can begin to think about the finances of your business. It doesn't have to be complex. You don't always need to be looking at "fancy" financial reports, although I encourage you to do so.

Documenting the details of what is coming in and what is going out enables you to ask educated questions about your business and evaluate it from a different perspective. It's not just about the amount of money you earn. The numbers give you a true picture of the overall financial health of your business, and they help signify the type of "financial nutrition" that is needed to help you reach your goals.

Conclusion

Now that you have read the book, you have a place to start. You have learned the importance of people, for you and your business. They are your greatest asset, from leveraging your strengths to investing in yourself as a leader and then developing a strong team around you for support.

You now have understanding of how to build a solid business foundation when it comes to planning, setting goals for your business, designing and orchestrating an exceptional client experience, and then documenting processes for your success.

You are capable of earning the salary you deserve by focusing your marketing efforts, leveraging a sales process and the financial data behind it, and evaluating that information. These are all tools and knowledge that accelerated my clinic growth and my success, and I am confident it will do the same for you.

Before we wrap up, let me offer you additional guidance:

- Business opportunities, challenges, and the environment around you always change. You want to continue to revisit and revise your plans and goals on a quarterly basis.
- Plan for the unexpected. What if you are taken away from your business for a day, week, or even a month or two? You need to consider having insurance to cover expenses

if you need to hire support while you are away. You want to document everything and know exactly who you can call in a time of need.

- Don't compare yourself to others. I see a lot of practitioners doing this. You want to celebrate your uniqueness and look for inspiration, not just within the industry, but also outside the industry.
- Your business should match and support your lifestyle, not necessarily be exactly like what others are doing.
- Love and respect our industry and support your colleagues. We are not competing with one another; there is more than enough work to go around.
- Take care of yourself. Business ownership is much more like a lifetime marathon than a sprint. You want to pace yourself and enjoy the ride.
- Seek the guidance and advice of mentors.
- Celebrate everything from your client's success to the milestones in your business and the opportunity to do what you love and make money at it.
- You can and should make the money your desire and deserve!
- When you align your passion with solid business skills, *you will be unstoppable.*

My Journey

Very early on, I adopted what I consider a simplified view of work and how people approached work in their lives. I believed everybody fell into one of two categories. Either you were the type of person who worked to make money, and that money allowed you to do what you loved, or you were the type of person who did what you loved and hopefully made some money in the process.

Being the action-oriented, high achiever that I was and still am, and starving for passion and meaning, I believed the second option was my most authentic choice.

I hurried through college, and then I secured a job in corporate America. There I climbed my way up the ladder taking on new roles and challenges and spent 15 years earning what I called an important title and making "good money." All the while, I was convincing myself I was passionate about whatever I was doing. With each new promotion, I found passion and vigor that urged me out of bed. However, it pushed me to overwork, and it drove me to keep going despite the tiny voice inside my head that said, "What am I doing all of this for?"

At some point, the voice became louder, and I began to see that I wasn't in the category I thought I was. I wasn't doing what I loved; I was working to make money by doing what I supposedly loved to do. The problem was, though I was making money, I wasn't prioritizing anything I loved doing anymore. I was a slave to my job, and I let the job define me.

This was when everything began to change. Hungry for true passion, I wanted to work for something and someone I believed in. I longed to feel connected; I wanted to be my true self on a daily basis without having to play a role.

Timing can be everything. By now, I had gained a higher level of self-confidence, and that was my true catalyst for change. This confidence, combined with a little bit of crazy and a whole lot of passion, ignited my decision.

My passion for holistic healthcare developed over time. I wasn't raised in a family where quality food was at the forefront, and there were times when my parents struggled just to put food on the table. I wasn't exposed to alternatives to Western medicine at a young age either. If I was sick, I went to the Western doctor, like everyone else I knew.

My brush with holistic practitioners didn't come until later when I was desperate, with no other options being presented to me.

From a very early age, I suffered from migraine headaches. This peaked during college when my daily headaches caused small seizures. I was also diagnosed with fibromyalgia. The series of pills I took made me feel no better, and the doctor said that I would grow out of it. I was desperate and depressed.

I managed to restore my health with nutritional changes and care from a variety of holistic practitioners. Through this process, the flame for holistic healthcare was sparked inside of me. I ignored it! After graduating with my Bachelor's degree, I secured for myself that exciting job that I was so passionate about in corporate America.

But you know how my journey unfolded. I ended up making the leap. I was 35 years old, and I had just finished my MBA program. Then I let go of everything I had worked for in corporate America to go back to school again for three years full time to follow my true passion in holistic health care. Did I mention that I have a little bit of crazy in me?

I let go of who I was to begin the process of becoming who I am meant to be. At the time, I thought that I should become an acupuncturist. My greatest dream after finishing acupuncture school was to start my own clinic. I wanted a clinic that integrated various practices within the field of holistic healthcare and brought practitioners in this field together. I believe we are much stronger together and that we can make a much greater impact in the whole field of healthcare this way.

I was able to accomplish my goal in less than two years. A two-year-old business is not mature, but I had created a solid foundation for my vision. The problem was that little voice inside of my head was still urging me to continue moving forward. My purpose and passion became much bigger than I initially dreamed for myself.

I love being a practitioner, and I am proud to be a Licensed Acupuncturist. Playing a role in the transformation of my clients' desperation into wellness is one of the greatest gifts I have received. As you know, a vast number of people suffer needlessly, even with endless options for care and alternatives to pharmaceuticals. There are wonderful practitioners, like you, who can help prevent and address minor symptoms before they become chronic diseases or facilitate the healing process of major health crises.

Eventually, I discovered that I am much more passionate about entrepreneurship than I thought. I am fiercely focused on demystifying alternative medicine for the global and general community by bringing practitioners within our industry to the forefront.

To accomplish my vision, I needed to move beyond being a Licensed Acupuncturist and deliver to you what has become second nature to me. Because when you align your passion with solid business skills, *you will be unstoppable.* This is my dream, and my role, within our industry.

Dear Reader,

To access your *Unstoppable* Resources, please go to

www.michellemcglade.com/unstoppableresources

Once there, you who have purchased my book will be able to request access to download companion worksheets and information for this book.

These tools are complimentary and as such customer support is limited.

Made in the USA
Lexington, KY
26 August 2018